Dear Dodie,
May GOD bless
you forever and ever.
Love you Precious Girl
6-19-23

THIS IS <u>NOT</u> THE END...

You can try again tomorrow!

by

JUDITH NEALY

With illustrations by
BILL SHURTLIFF

WestBow Press books may be ordered through booksellers or by contacting:

WestBow Press
A Division of Thomas Nelson & Zondervan
1663 Liberty Drive
Bloomington, IN 47403
www.westbowpress.com
1 (866) 928-1240

Cover and Interior Illustrations by Bill Shurtliff

ISBN: 978-1-4908-5355-0 (sc)
ISBN: 978-1-4908-5356-7 (e)

Library of Congress Control Number: 2014917189

Printed in the United States of America.

WestBow Press rev. date: 11/06/2014

WESTBOW*
PRESS
A DIVISION OF THOMAS NELSON
& ZONDERVAN

For my ANGELS on earth

Mari

Jacob & Luke

Jeremiah

For my ANGEL already in Heaven

Betty Jean Lagow

Beatrice Jean is a caterpillar. She is a rather unusual caterpillar because she has a pony tail that sticks straight up on the top of her head.

She lives on the window ledge of the old church at 825 Chestnut Street with her mother. Her grandmother lives at 829 on the very same street.

Beatrice Jean is so excited today. This is a day greater than all days. She is going to see her grandmother.

She closed her eyes and imagined how she and Grandmother would bake cupcakes and walk through the garden to pick flowers for the table. Then they would have a cup of tea.

"Grandmother always has a beautiful present for me, too. The presents are always wrapped in sparkly paper with shiny bows," she said. "I just love them."

She squeezed her eyes shut very, very tight and tried to imagine what would be inside. "I just can't wait," and she SQUEALED right out loud.

Days with Grandmother are always the best. Beatrice Jean loves her grandmother very much and cannot wait to hug her.

Hugging Grandmother makes her feel all warm and cozy inside. Hugging Grandmother was kinda like putting on a new winter coat and mittens and getting all snuggled and warm.

Today, Mother said that Beatrice Jean was a big girl and that she could walk alone to Grandmother's house. It wasn't far, and they had gone there many times before.

She was SO excited to be a big girl. If she stood on her tippy-toes she could see Grandmother's house right from her window ledge.

She would do a good job and make Mama proud of her. "Yep, yep, yep," she said. "This is the best day ever."

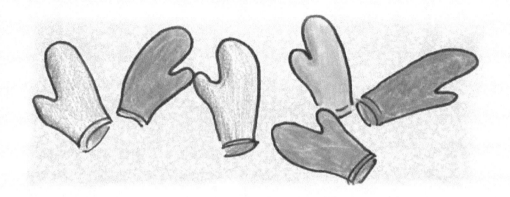

Beatrice Jean got her backpack from the closet and put ALL of her garden boots in it. They would be good for the walk in the garden to pick flowers for the table at Grandmother's house.

AND she put ALL of her oven mitts in her backpack, too. They would be good for taking the cupcakes out of the oven.

And then she and Grandmother would have a cup of tea. And they would use pretty little napkins that said "THIS IS A SPECIAL DAY" on them.

Mama was a little nervous, but Beatrice Jean was SO excited.

She put on her backpack, and she and Mama held hands to say a prayer for her safety as she traveled to Grandmother's house alone for the very first time.

Mama said, "God will keep you safe." Beatrice Jean believed it, too. God would keep her safe. She was

not at all worried. This was going to be a wonderful day. This was going to be a very special day. This was going to be the BEST DAY EVER.

Beatrice Jean turned around several times and waved at Mama as she inched her way down the path that she and Mama had traveled along so many times before.

She had a big smile on her face, and her pony tail was extra perky. She was SO excited. Nothing was going to spoil this day. Nothing was going to spoil this feeling in her happy, happy heart.

Beatrice Jean's World

Beatrice Jean had not gone far when she came upon her good friends, the three little squirrels. "I'm going to my grandmother's house," she said. "We will have tea and cupcakes, and my grandmother will have a present for me."

She and her friends giggled. They said, "Isn't the sunshine beautiful today?" And then they said, "Good bye," and Beatrice Jean started on her way again. She was SO excited. Her friends were excited, too, and they waved and waved until Beatrice Jean disappeared out of sight.

She had not gone much farther when she came upon three more of her good friends, the three little birds. "I'm going to my grandmother's house," she said. "We will have tea and cupcakes, and Grandmother will have a present for me.

She and her friends giggled. They said, "Isn't the sunshine beautiful today?" And then they said, "Good bye," and Beatrice Jean started on her way again. She was SO excited. Her friends were excited, too. And they waved and waved as she disappeared out of sight.

Beatrice Jean had not gone much farther when she came upon three more of her good friends, the three bumble bees. "I'm going to my grandmother's house," she said. "We will have tea and cupcakes, and my grandmother will have a present for me."

She and her friends giggled. They said, "Isn't the sunshine beautiful today?" And they said, "Good bye," and Beatrice Jean started on her way again. She was SO excited. Her friends were excited, too, and they waved and they waved as she disappeared out of sight.

Beatrice Jean had not gone much farther when she came upon a very shocking situation. The pony tail on the top of her head stood straight up in the air.
"Why, my goodness," she said. The path to Grandmother's house was blocked by a stream of water, and she could not swim.

She was SO confused. It's true. The sunshine was beautiful today. Everyone had noticed that. But it had rained yesterday and the day before. Now, there was water in places that water should not be. A LOT of water.

Beatrice Jean walked back and forth on the path for several minutes. "I can see Grandmother's house from here, but there is no way that I can get there. What should I do?" she said. "What should I do?" she said again.

Then she saw a rather smallish, medium-sized, very leafy tree standing just on the other side of the water that was blocking her way to Grandmothers house.

She got SO excited. She had a great idea. "I will pray and ask God to let that smallish tree fall across the water that is blocking my way. Then I will crawl across the tree and be on my way. And I will have my tea and cupcakes, and I will get my present."

So Beatrice Jean lifted her face towards Heaven and sincerely asked God to please let the rather smallish,

medium-sized, very leafy tree fall across the water that was blocking her way to Grandmother's house. She said, "I do want my tea. I do want my cupcakes, and I do want my present. But most of all, I want to hug my grandmother."

Beatrice Jean paced back and forth along the little path. She looked and looked for another way to cross the water, but there was none. Back and forth. Back and forth. Looking. Looking. Looking.

After several long minutes she prayed again. She asked God to please let the rather smallish, medium-sized, leafy tree fall across the water that was blocking her way to Grandmother's house. She said, "I do want my present. I do want my cupcakes. I do want my present. I do want to hug my grandmother." She was beginning to feel disappointed.

She finally sat down. AT A VERY SAFE DISTANCE FROM THE WATER. And she waited. She waited again. And she waited some more.

Finally, she took ALL the boots out of her backpack, and she tried them ALL on. It would be so much fun to go in the garden and pick flowers with Grandmother. She sighed. A very big sigh. And then she took them ALL off and put them carefully back in her bag.

Once more, she sat down. AT A VERY SAFE DISTANCE FROM THE WATER. And she waited. She waited again. And she waited some more. Finally, she took out ALL of the oven mitts from her backpack, and she tried them ALL on. It would be so much fun to go in the kitchen with Grandmother and bake cupcakes. She sighed. A very big sigh. And then she took them ALL off and put them carefully back into her bag.

Then she sat down. AT A VERY SAFE DISTANCE FROM THE WATER. And she waited. She waited again. And she waited some more.

It is true. The sunshine had been very beautiful today. But it was starting to fade, just a little. It was no longer the early hours of the morning, and the rather smallish, medium-sized, very leafy tree was still standing straight and tall by the water that blocked her way to Grandmother's house. Now, she was very disappointed.

She put her backpack on. She sighed. A very big sigh. She had decided to go home.

Before going very far, Beatrice Jean came upon three of her friends, the bumble bees. "Why are you coming home so soon?" said the bumble bees. So, Beatrice Jean told them her story and how God had not answered her prayer to let the rather smallish, medium-sized, very leafy green tree fall. "OH NO! OH NO!" shouted the bumble bees. "Our grandmother lives in that tree."

"Well," said Beatrice Jean, "The tree did not fall." The little bumble bees lifted their wings toward heaven and cheered. They were SO happy. "Thank you, God, for keeping our grandmother safe," they shouted. And they buzzed and they buzzed and they buzzed.

Before going much farther, Beatrice Jean again
came upon her three friends, the little birds.
"Why are you coming home so soon?" said the
little birds. So, Beatrice Jean told them her
story and how God did not answer her prayer
to let the rather smallish, medium-sized, leafy
tree fall. "OH NO,
OH NO," shouted
the little birds.
"Our grandmother
lives in that tree.
We asked God to
keep her safe
today. We love our
grandmother."

"Well," said
Beatrice Jean,
"The tree did not
fall." The little
birds lifted their wings toward heaven and
cheered and cheered. They were SO happy.
"Thank you, God, for keeping our grandmother
safe," they shouted, and they chirped and they
chirped and they chirped.

Before going much farther, Beatrice Jean came upon  three more of her friends, the little squirrels. "Why are you coming home so soon?" said the little squirrels. So, Beatrice Jean told them her story and how God had not answered her prayer to let the rather smallish, medium-sized, leafy tree fall. "OH NO, OH NO," shouted the three little squirrels. "Our grandmother lives in that tree. We asked God to keep her safe today."

"Well," said Beatrice Jean, "The tree did not fall." The three little squirrels lifted their tiny hands toward heaven and cheered and cheered. "We love our grandmother," they said. They were SO happy. "Thank you, God, for keeping our grandmother safe," they shouted. And they cheered and they cheered and they cheered.

Beatrice Jean finally made her way home to Mama.
She ran to Mama's arms and told her the story of
her day.

She told Mama how the difficult stream of water
had caused her to pray and ask God to make the
rather smallish, medium-sized, leafy tree fall so she
could safely crawl across it and see Grandmother.

And how the little squirrels and the little birds and how the little bees ALL had grandmothers that lived in that very tree. And how they all had prayed that God would keep their grandmothers safe.

"They love their grandmothers just like I love mine," she said.

Mama gently hugged Beatrice Jean for a long time. They were both SO happy that God always knows best.

They said, "Thank you, God, for keeping everyone safe today."

Then Mama said to Beatrice Jean,

"Today is not
THE END
You can try again tomorrow."

Beatrice Jean and Mama looked up
towards heaven and they smiled. They
wrapped their arms around each other.
It was like putting on a new winter coat
and mittens and getting all snuggled
and warm.

Proverbs 3: 5-6
Trust in the Lord with all your heart and
lean not unto your own understanding.
In all your ways acknowledge Him
and He shall direct your paths.

CPSIA information can be obtained
at www.ICGtesting.com
Printed in the USA
LVHW012259130623
749721LV00008B/187